How to Create a Website

Get web presence & stand out in today's competitive employment marketplace

By: Jenny Aaron

Step 1: Name Your Website

Step 2: Register your Domain Name
　　　2 Places where I buy my domain names from

Step 3: Find Hosting

Step 4: Connect your Domain Name with your Web Host

Step 5: Quick Install WordPress & Set Up Your
　　　WebSite Familiarize Yourself With WordPress

　Step 6: Change Your Permalink Structure

　Step 7: Create your About Me Page
　　　How to setup your "About Me" Page on a Personal Website

　Step 8: Add your Contact Form
　　　Now Everything is Coming Along Nicely

　Step 9: Select your WordPress Theme

　Step 10: Installing Your WordPress Theme (No Need to use FTP!)

　Step 11: Add Some Much Needed Plugins and Widgets
　　　Let's Add Some Widgets!
　　　Congratulations You Have a Fully Built Website!

This guide is for you if you are....

-> Someone who wants to learn how to create your own website from scratch without spending thousands of dollars on fancy software or web designers.

-> Looking to have a web presence your own professional industry-specific business such as: Yoga instructor, life coach, consultant etc.

-> Someone who wants to start a hobby blog in areas such as a fashion, cooking, internet marketing etc.

-> A recent graduate applying for jobs and entering the grown-up job market.

-> A freelance writer, graphic designer, web designer, financial consultant etc. and are looking to establish your name and gain exposure in order to attract clients.

-> A photographer setting up your own photography website to showcase your work and establish your online presence

The employment marketplace is a competitive place. So whether you work for somebody else or work for yourself the competition is always there. Gone are the days where your credentials and education solely guaranteed you a job. These days you will need to think creatively in order to get the job. Whether you are a freelance writer, yoga instructor, or someone looking to get your foot through the door of corporate America. Having a website is essential. It enables you to let your personality and your work shine. Your website is important because it is what will help you to differentiate yourself from the crowd.

To most people, the idea of creating their very own blog or website is daunting and intimidating to say the least. Many of us picture the days of having to learn complicated code and HTML in order to setup a simple web page and get online. - This could not be further from the truth! If you are looking to **start a blog or personal website**,it is not as complicated as you might think and no, you absolutely do not need to know how to code or learn HTML to get started! Why should you setup your own blog or personal website? **Having an online presence is very important in the job market and can act as the one thing that sets you apart from other job applicants in the competitive job market. -**Plus starting a blog or setting up your very own personal website is easy!

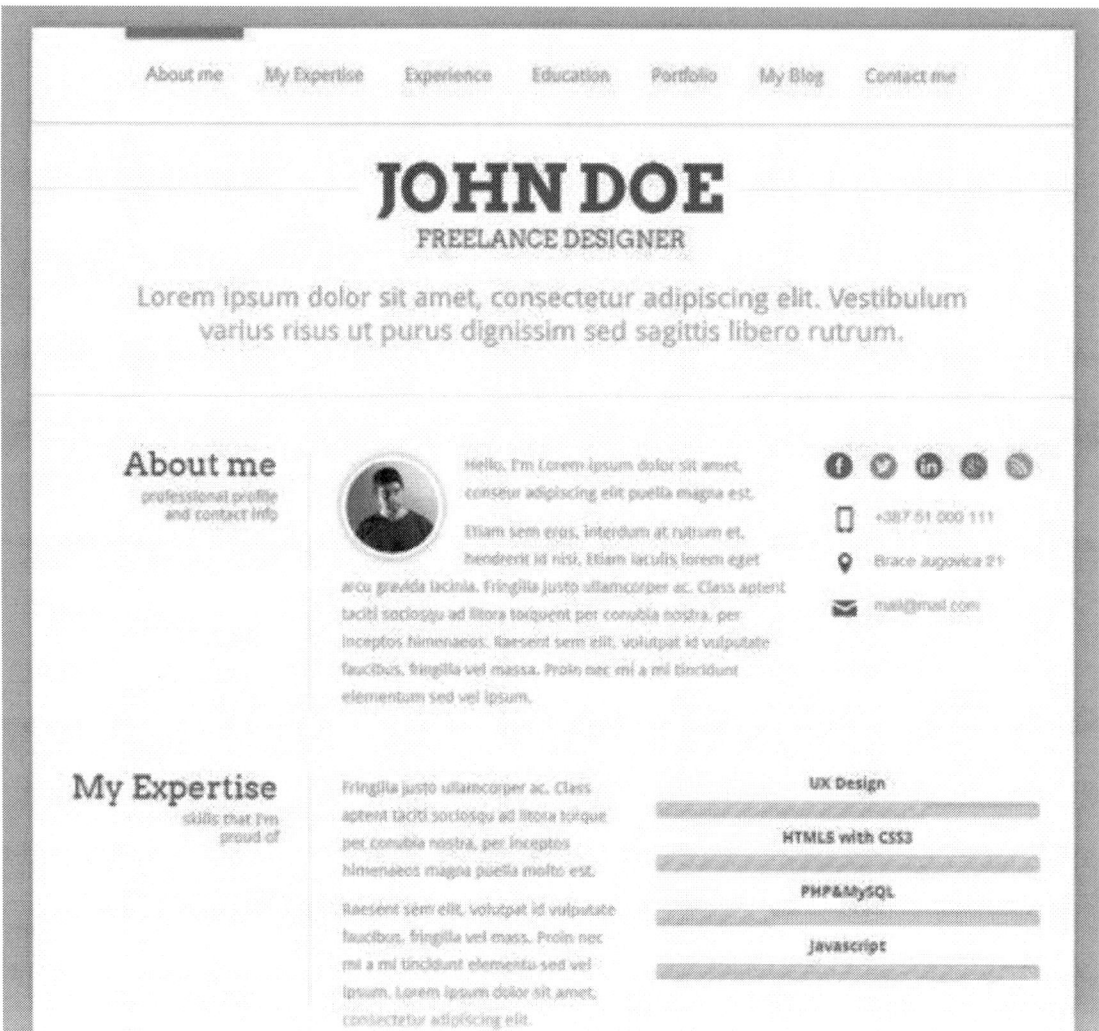

Picture this, you and 100 other people apply for a job position and out of those 100 people, around 25 are chosen for an interview. Out of the 25 candidates interviewed, only 15 qualify for a second interview, and out of these 15 people, only two have an online presence achieved by owning and running their very own personal website /blog. This is the one thing that differentiates them (aside from their Linkedin profiles) from the herd. Now which person do you think is most likely to peak the interest of the interview: The person who just presents themselves as yet another job applicant or the person who has something more going for them such as an online presence? Hmmm...I will let you answer this for yourself.

6 Reasons You Need to Setup a Personal Website or Start a Blog

1.) **You get to control what other people can find about you online.** If people Google your name usually all they can find are your social media profiles such as your Twitter, or Facebook (if you use your real name that is...) and sometimes your Linkedin profile (if you have one). But when you have your own personal website/blog, it is likely to be among the top results in any search engine

2.) **You make yourself instantly interesting.** When people find your personal website/blog online, they are inclined to think 'hmmm... Who is this person? What is his/her website about?... **Let me click over and see what they have to say/offer**'

3.) **Stand out from the crowd.** Having a blog/website allows you to stand out and differentiate yourself. Even though there are millions of blogs in the interwebs today, keep in mind that people with blogs do not blog in identical niches/topics. If anyone tells you 'There are way too many personal finance blogs, the web does not need another!' Ignore this hater (they probably suffer from extreme indigestion anyways) and instead start your own personal finance blog and give and add your own unique flare!

4.) **Pass on something of value to your readers** Having your own website/blog, can help you to communicate and offer valuable information and this in turn can help you to showcase your work/talents to potential employers or partners by providing them with a window to see what you are capable of. - Oh and did I mention sharing can earn you online karma points for the future!

5) **It allows you to network...COMFORTABLY.** Whenever I think of networking, I picture a room filled with people suited up in their best business wear armed with business cards and making super awkward small talk then randomly handing out their business cards without making any real connection to one another.
With blogging you actually get the chance to build and form a relationship with your readers as well as with other bloggers. You get to know them by commenting on their blogs, participating in podcasts and even collaborating on projects.

6.) ***You get to be the creator of something.*** There's something satisfying about taking an idea from concept to life. Starting your own blog is no different as it will gives you a sense of purpose and community to be able have something you are working towards in life, even if it's something you do once a week or frequently.

For the above industries, you can showcase your blog or website to potential clients in many ways: If you are a photographer, having an online portfolio can help you to showcase the quality of your work to potential clients/employers. You can impress clients or a potential employer as an interior decorator/designer by having an online blog full of pictures of past projects. Allow your clients to see your talents as a web designer by pointing them to your online web design portfolio of past work you have done. If you are looking to build your business as a fitness trainer, why not start a blog with a main focus on exercise & nutrition as well as display your past work with client's before and after pictures (just be sure to ask their permission first)...The list goes on. A blog or personal website can act as the avenue to help you get hired, build a business, get connected, attract opportunities and differentiate yourself from the pack...But only if you finally GET OFF YOUR BUTT AND START!

So you want to setup a personal website or start a blog?....

What you do Not need to know
- Complicated HTML of any other complex code that would otherwise look gibberish
- Photoshop, Dreamweaver or any other

Here is what you will learn with this guide?
1. How to register a domain name
2. How to get hosting
3. Places to get an awesome and attractive theme for your website
4. Essential must have plugins to secure, optimize and seamlessly run your blog/website

Full Disclosure: *If you decide to use the hosting and domain options I recommend within this guide and you click on any of my links in order to get the product, I will earn a commission (it will not cost you anything and it can even cost you less because i can provide you with coupon code or two). If you choose to get your domain name or hosting through my link, I want to thank you as it is my aim that this tutorial will help you get started online.*

Step 1: Name Your Website

The first thing you want to do is come up with a name for your blog or website. When coming up with a name, make sure that it's easy to remember and complementary to your industry of choice or niche. If you are setting up a personal website then your first and last name will suffice. The main point is, you need to pick a name that you like and feel is suitable for whatever it is that you would like to accomplish. -So whether that means registering fitbodiesunite.com or queenofcupcakes.com, - or whatever comes to mind.

Step 2: Register your Domain Name

The next thing you will want to do is to pick the right domain for your website. If it's your goal to have you very own personal website, then you probably want to go with a name like firstandlastname.com. If the name you want is taken, you will have to improvise by placing a middle initial in the middle or come up with a different name. With a blog you can get more creative, (think short and sweet).

2 Places where I buy my domain names from

There are many places where you can buy your domain name from online, however I only use the following two companies:

Namecheap.com :This is also a good place to buy domain names, their .com's start at $10.69/year.

Godaddy.com:Their domain names are fairly priced and they even have a promotion right now where you can get domains for as little as $8.99 .
I really like Godaddy because you can usually get coupons with them, whereas as much as I also like Namecheap, as a company they do not offer coupons, however the domain name registration atNamecheapdoes come with a free '**Who is**'protection option that you can activate in the case that you do not want anybody to lookup your website domain name and be able to see your address and who the owner is.

Word of advice ->In case you find a domain that you really really want for your blog or website, register it immediately because you just might search for it the next day and somebody else could have snapped it up (believe me, I learned the hard way). -Oh and it's probably not a good idea to register a name such as crazyforcocopuffs982-29.com!

It is VERY important to have a good domain name. I do not think this fact can be stressed enough.

If you are setting up a personal website your domain name can be in the structure of **Yourfirstlastname.com**and there you can include a portfolio of your past work and links to all the social media profiles where you can be found as well as a link to your company website and main blog if you own a company or run a blog.

Avoid this when setting up a domain name:
- Using numbers in your domain name
- Using dashes, only use them if you absolutely have to.
- Making your domain name longer than three words (it's too long)
- Using super complicated and hard to spell domain names
- Avoid domain names with extensions such as .biz, .info they can be spammy looking.
- Make sure if you are using wording found in the dictionary to SPELL the name correctly!

Remember, the main goal here is to make it as easy and as simple as possible for people to find your website. Did you know nowadays you can buy your domain name in the same place you get your hosting from? It will cost you around $4 more but if you want the convenience, this is an option you are free to pursue.

After you have come up with a good domain name, you are now ready to get your hosting.

Step 3: Find Hosting

The second thing you need to consider is whether you want a self hosted or a free website on WordPress or Blogger such as one with the extension Yourwebsite.wordpress.com or Yourwebsite.blogpost.com, the end decision is really up to you. If you are on a very strict budget, there is nothing wrong with starting off with a free website at WordPress.com or Blogger.com

In my own personal opinion I believe that having a self hosted website/blog looks waaaay better and more presentable, - especially if you want to develop a strong brand and be taken more seriously in your industry.

Reliable website hosting is not free, however, it is worth considering since it offers many benefits in the long run.

There are thousands upon thousands of web hosts on the Internet and the options you can choose to go with are endless. Since I am happy whenever I pay a reasonable price for stuff that actually works, I am going to make an assumption that this is also the case with most of my readers as well.

So what type of website hosting is the best? It really depends on the type of website you want to run but since this tutorial is about **how you can start a blog or personal website from start to finish**, I will just keep things as uncomplicated and as focused as possible.

My top choice for web hosting is the Just Host shared hosting package, I have been consistently using Just Host since 2008 and have never experienced any serious problems with their product or service.

Justhost hosting plans are very reasonably priced and affordable, plus they do not have any downtime and the best thing about their hosting plan is they provide a WordPress Quick Install option (if you ever need to start a blog on WordPress, it's a breeze!)

In late 2012 one of my websites was affected by a Malware that made every one of my live posts super wonky (I am talking all different types of codes were showing up that I could not decipher and I was frazzled, angry and had tried everything on my own to resolve the issue), when I contacted Justhost, the first agent I spoke to was unable to help me to completely resolve the issue, however what I didn't know was that he had submitted a ticket to have a higher level agent look into the issue.

I went to bed kind of frustrated and close to pulling out most of my hair from the scalp! But lo and behold the very next day when I woke up, I saw an email saying that 2 tickets had been opened and also my issue was resolved, my website was FULLY RESTORED to full working order and I have never had another issue since then. So what was the issue? Justhost support told me what had affected my computer was Malware from using an infected computer! (a warning for everybody, do not use any unknown computers to access and work on your blog!)

You can use the coupon code **letsgoweb** to get a percentage off your first hosting purchase. . With this coupon you actually save more when you would if you just used the Justhost default signup.
*Please note:*These instructions can be applied for use with any other hosting provider and are not restricted for use with Justhost.

Justhost has 3 plans: Starter $5.99/month, Plus $9.99/month and Business Pro $19.99/month Once you have decided on the type of plan you want.

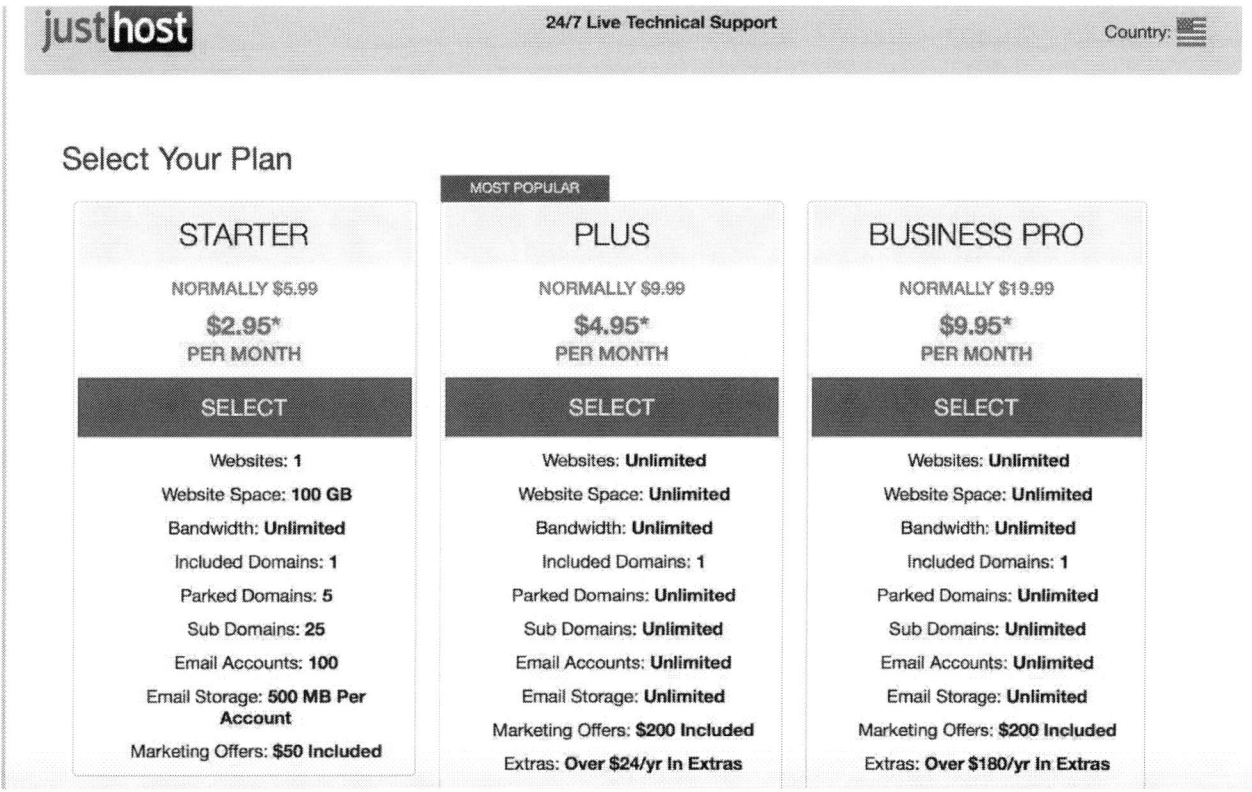

At the time of the screenshot, Justhost was having a summer sale *prices subject to change

After you have made payment, you'll receive an email with all the information you'll need to continue.

Step 4: Connect your Domain Name with your Web Host

Now that you have both your domain name and your hosting setup, you will need to get your domain name and your hosting account connected to one another. How do you do this? It's simple really, all you have to do change the domain name servers (also known as DNS). I do not want to get all technical, but the easiest way to explain a DNS and web host connection is to think of the DNS as the zip code and your domain name as the main address. If the DNS is a 90210, then all mail needs to be routed to Beverly Hills since 90210 is the Beverly Hills zip code. So if you were to mail something to someone in this location, you would need to use the 90210 zip code otherwise if you put down any zip code the mail may not get there since it will not go to the right zip code! ***Here's how you change your domain name DNS to your web host***

You will get an email welcome message from your web host providing you with the DNS details that you will need in order to change your DNS on your domain name to match those of your web host cPanel.

1. Log into your hosting account's cPanel and scroll down to the bottom and you will see numbers that look sort of like: NS1.SLICEHOST.NET and NS1.SLICEHOST.NET (*it won't say slicehost.com this is just an imaginary company!*)

2. Copy the domain nameservers from step 1

3. Now Sign in to your Godaddy or Namecheap Account Manager

4. Choose **'Manage Domains'** option and select the domain you want to modify.

5. From the **Nameservers** menu choose the **'Manage'** option

6. Under **Setup Type** select **'Custom'**

7. Click on **'Edit Nameservers'** link and paste the Nameservers you got in step #1 and hit **'Save'**

The end result should look similar to:

Set Nameservers

If you are hosting your Web site with us (you have a hosting account with us associated with this domain) or you want to Park or Forward your domain, we will automatically set your nameservers for you.

- ○ I want to **park** my domains.
- ○ I want to **forward** my domains.
- ○ I have a **hosting account** with these domains.
- ● I have **specific nameservers** for my domains.

Nameserver 1: *	Nameserver 2: *	Nameserver 3:
NS1.SLICEHOST.NET	NS2.SLICEHOST.NET	NS3.SLICEHOST.NET

Add more | Manage DS Records   **OK** Cancel

Step 5: Quick Install WordPress & Set Up Your WebSite

Here is where you actually begin to build your website/blog.

In this tutorial, you will be using a self-hosted WordPress to setup your website, not WordPress.com. Keep in mind you have endless choices as to which types of websites you can setup with WordPress so do not feel limited by thinking you can only set up blog sites. If you wanted to, you can setup a company website, personal website, eCommerce site, portfolio site etc.

The best thing about WordPress is it only takes around 5 minutes or less to install! How is this so? You can do this through the WordPress Quick-Install offered by your hosting company.

Steps you will need to take:

1. Login to your Hosting account's cPanel. You can login by typing in this URL into your Internet browser: **yourdomainame.com/cpanel**(of course you want to replace yourdomainame with your actual domain name) If your domain name is taking too long to reach, you can make use of the link JustHost sent you in the first registration email.

Please note: If you are working with more than one domain name, you will need to click on "**Add on Domains**"also located in the front end of cPanel under the tab with the heading '***Domains***'and add your domain name to cPanel before you can install WordPress with QuickInstall

3. You will now be directed to the front end of your cPanel. In order to install WordPress, you will want to get near the bottom of the page and there you will see a link for Quick Install.

4. Click on 'Quick Install' link located on the homepage underneath the 'Software and Services' tab

5. Once you get inside the "QuickInstall" on the left hand side you will see a 'WordPress button, click that

6. Select the domain name you want to develop a WordPress site for and fill in the information required such as the website's username, site tag line, and your email (so you can get the login details emailed to you)

In the Quickinstall area you want to click on the button labelled "Install WordPress"

Enter all your information and remember to put in the right email so that you can receive your login details!

Install WordPress

Fill out the form below to get started with your install.

| ▼ | / | install/path/here |

Admin Email

Blog Title

Admin User

First Name

Last Name

[Install WordPress]

By clicking install/import above, you accept our Terms of Service agreement.

Please note:it can sometimes take up to 2 hours for your web host to set your account up. You may be able to access your cPanel almost instantly, however your domain name may not be accessible for up to 2 hours.

Pat yourself on the back, you have just installed WordPress in 5 minutes or lessand you should now have a fully functioning website!

Before we move on to creating posts, setting up pages, installing plugins etc, let us first take a look at WordPress itself and get a feel for the Dashboard and define what's what.

Familiarize Yourself With WordPress

WordPress is a Content Management System (CMS) that is relatively easy to navigate and use. If you want to know more about it, there's even a tutorial feature as long as you have the latest 3.3+ version of WP installed. Below are a few key terms to remember:

- **Dashboard** -This is the "hub page" of WordPress. The Dashboard is what you will see once you log in each and every time.
- **Posts** – Here is where you will go each time you want to write up a blog post or edit any other already published posts.
- **Media** –Any pictures you upload, videos, or any kind of media can be located and viewed here.
- **Pages** – Here you can create the pages that will show up in your website's main navigation. With the 'pages' option you can add your about me page, contact page, sitemap etc.
- **Comments** - Ifanybody (human/computer) comments on your blog, you will be able to see them here (you can also disable the comments).
- **Appearance** –You can customize your website's look and feel via the appearance menu by using customized menus, widgets and you can also edit your theme code.
- Plugins – Manage your plugins and give your website more functionality by adding the necessary plugins
- **Users** -You can change your website password here.
- **Tools** -Import/Export blog content here. You will rarely need to use this menu options.
- **Settings** – This particular area has a lot of stuff from your permalinks, reading, writing and so much more.

Now that you have an idea on the functionality in the dashboard, you will have an easier time creating and navigating your website.

Now do not forget to do this important yet very simple thing…

Step 6: Change Your Permalink Structure

Whenever you create a post or a page, WordPress will just create a generic default URL similar to the following: **yourdomain.com/?p=123**. This is a very ugly URL and definitely something you do not want.
With a properly structured permalink your url for your 'About Me' page will look like **yourdomain.com/aboutme**. Now this is what you want.

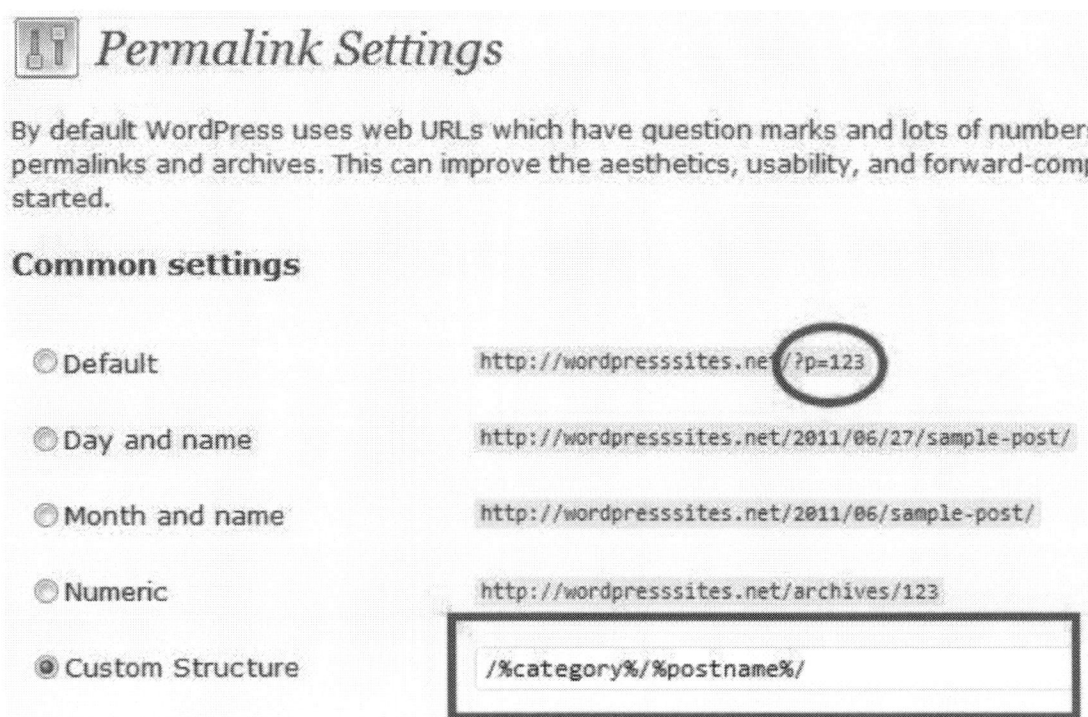

In order to do this, you will need to adjust your permalink structure. This is very straightforward and much cleaner and nicer than the default URL.
1. Go over to the **Settings** link and click on on the **Permalinks**
2. Select the **Post Name** option
3. Format your permalinks as: **/%postname%/**
4. Save the changes.

Having a well structured permalink gives your post URL a clean and put together look and takes less than a second to do!

Step 7: Create your About Me Page

Now onto building pages...

Pages are static and will always stay on your website so all that a person has to do is click on the tab to link to a page you've posted. Posts will move down the page with every new blog post published.

Do you really need to create pages? I would have to say yes you do. Why? It makes you more unique and interesting and provides additional information that will always be easily findable via your website's top tabs.

There is a selection of pages you should build especially if you choose to start and maintain a personal website. These include:

- An **About Me** page is usually the first thing people want to see when they come to your website.
- A further detailed **Biography** page
- A **Past Work** page (if you are building a business/personal website)
- A **Contact** page that will disclose how people can get in touch with you. You will need to add a contact form for this.

Other pages you probably want to add, (but only if they fit your needs):

- A **Portfolio**-This will allow you to showcase any of the work you have done, - this can be anything from content writing, graphic design, web design, interior design etc. You can create this any which way you want, although you may find a theme that is portfolio ready much more suitable.
- A **Hire Me** page- I would strongly suggest to have this as an active page especially if you are a freelance writer, designer or are aspiring to start looking for freelance work. This page itself will tell people what you are looking to do and why you are the best fit for the job.
- A **Press** page - If you have ever been featured or mentioned and you would like to share this with the world, feel free to do so, - after all, it helps your credibility!

The decision is yours when it comes to deciding the kinds of pages you would like to have on your website. I am however going to walk you through on how to create an **About Me** page, and from there you can follow the same steps in order to create the rest.

Make sure that you delete the default WordPress sample page and sample post that are come with your initial website installation. All you have to do is find the post labelled as "**Hello World**"and "**Sample Page**"and send them to the Trash.

When creating your "About Me" Page...

Remember your About Me page is a page that many of your visitors will at one point see. It is also a page that you want to make as interesting as you possibly can. This page will include a short summary of what your website or blog is about, who you are, what you do/study, and where you work or how you make a living. It's also awesome to have a picture or two of yourself and if you are a freelancer, web designer etc. it would be a bonus to have a few words or quotes about your work from past or current clients.

How to setup your "About Me" Page on a Personal Website

Since we are creating a personal website as opposed to a blog, the first page you will want your site visitors to see is your **About Me**page, so it only makes sense to set it up as your main home page!

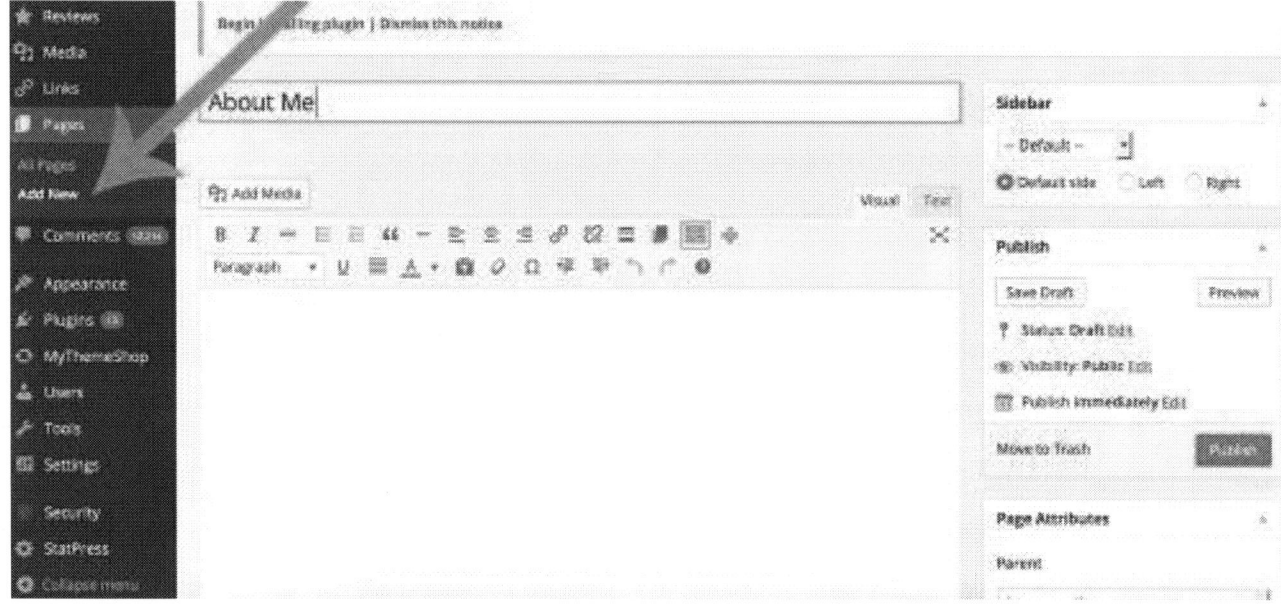

Reading Settings

Front page displays
- ○ Your latest posts
- ● A static page (select below)
  - Front page: About
  - Posts page: — Select —

Blog pages show at most 12 posts

Syndication feeds show the most recent 10 items

For each article in a feed, show
- ● Full text
- ○ Summary

Search Engine Visibility ☐ Discourage search engines from indexing this site
It is up to search engines to honor this request.

[Save Changes]

1. On the left dashboard sidebar, scroll down and hover over the **Settings** option, then click on **Reading**.
2. Where it says **Front Page Displays** click on the button that reads **A Static Page**
3. Select your **About Me** page as the main home page.
4. In the case that you would like a blog on your personal website, all you have to do is to publish a blank page and name it **Blog**, then set this up as the Posts Page
5. Save all your changes.

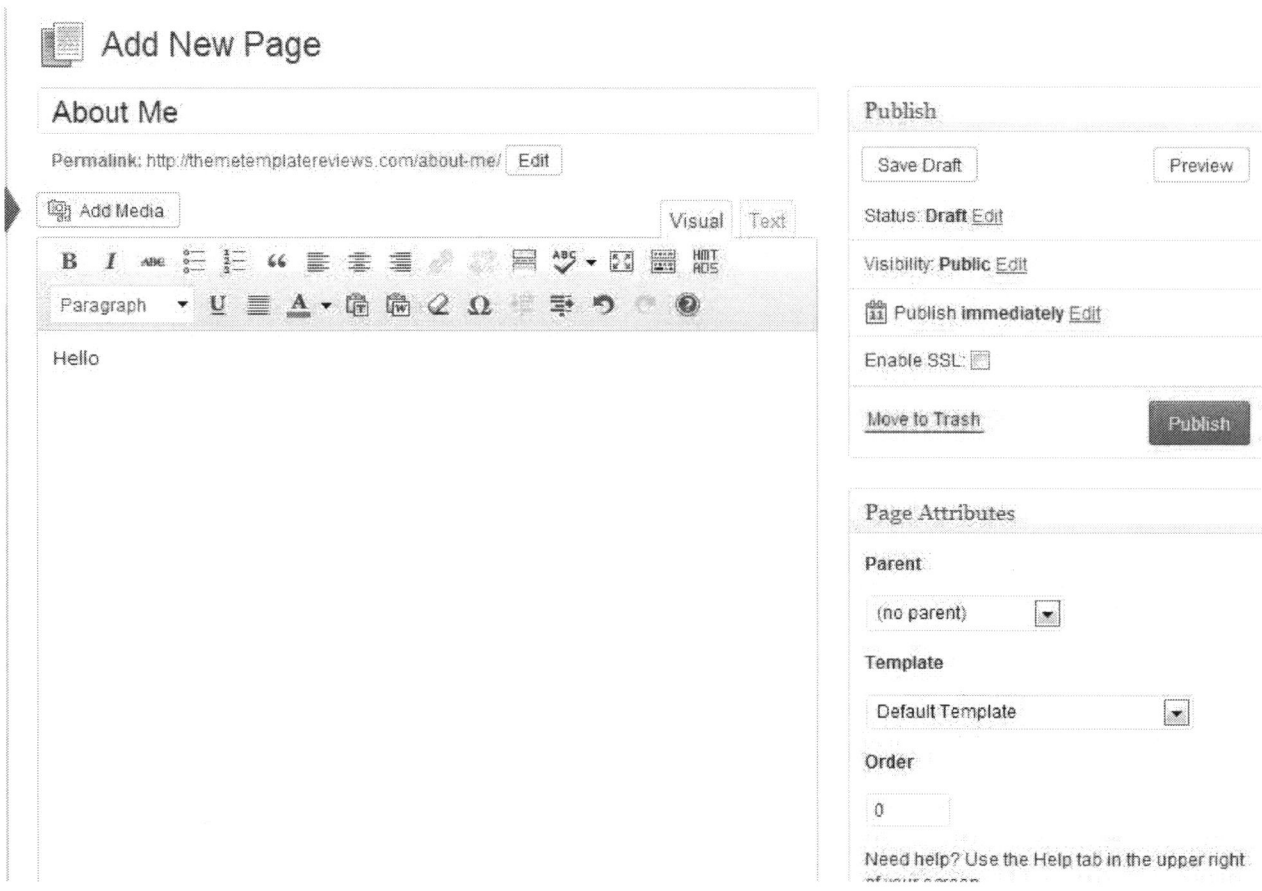

If you want your 'About Me' page to be the first thing people see, set it as a static page, otherwise if you are creating your website to be a blog, skip this step and leave '*static page*'unchecked and instead select your front page to be '***Your Latest Posts***'

Now you can add some content to your **About Me** page...

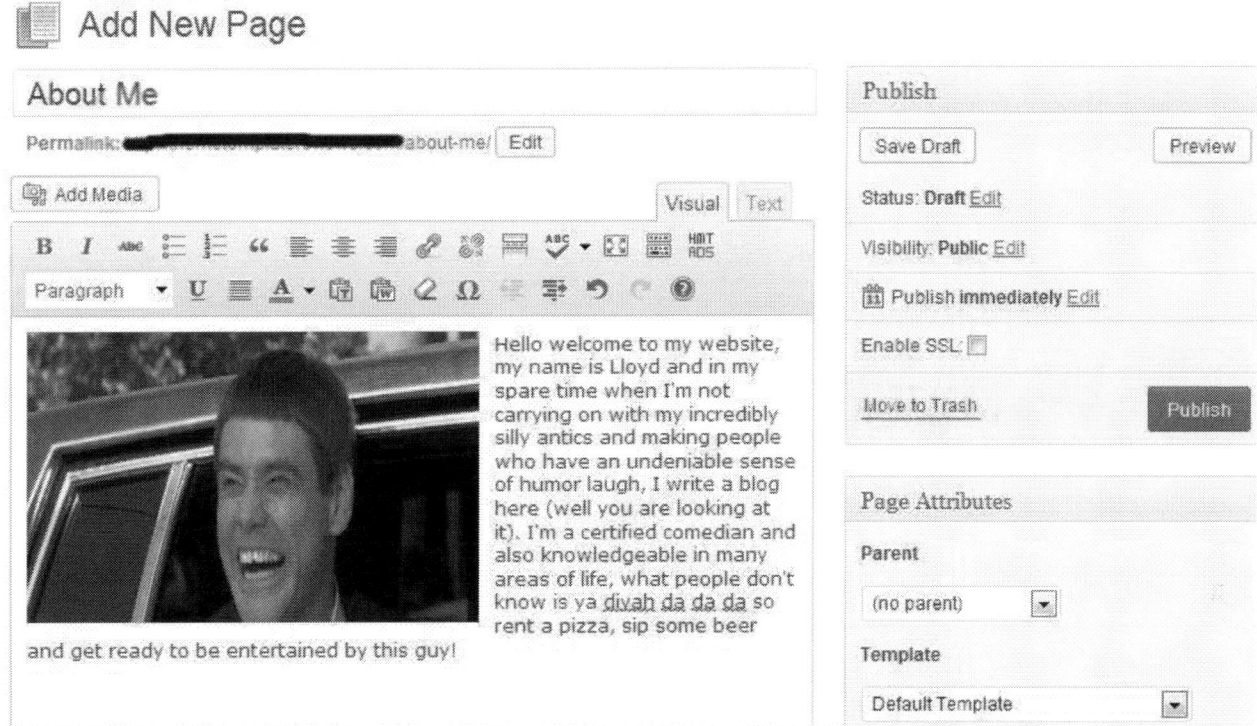

If you're a professional such as an accountant, consultant, lawyer etc. you probably want to put up a picture of you looking the part. Easy peezy you get the idea!

Step 8: Add your Contact Form

It's important to add a contact form to your website, whether you have a personal website or a blog. Having a contact form on your website allows for anybody who reads your blog or views your personal website to send an inquiry, ask questions and be able to communicate with you privately You can add a contact form by either buying a WordPress theme that already comes with a built-in contact form or installing one by using a plugin. I usually just use a plugin for all my contact forms, my plugin of choice is the Fast Secure Contact Form WordPress plugin. It's free of charge and easy to install and configure,- all you have to do is **Add a New Page**, name the page **Contact Us/ Contact Me/Get in Touch** etc, then you can paste the plugin shortcode and click publish. If you are a freelancer, you can also make use of the secure Contact Form Plugin by using it on your **Hire Me** page.

22

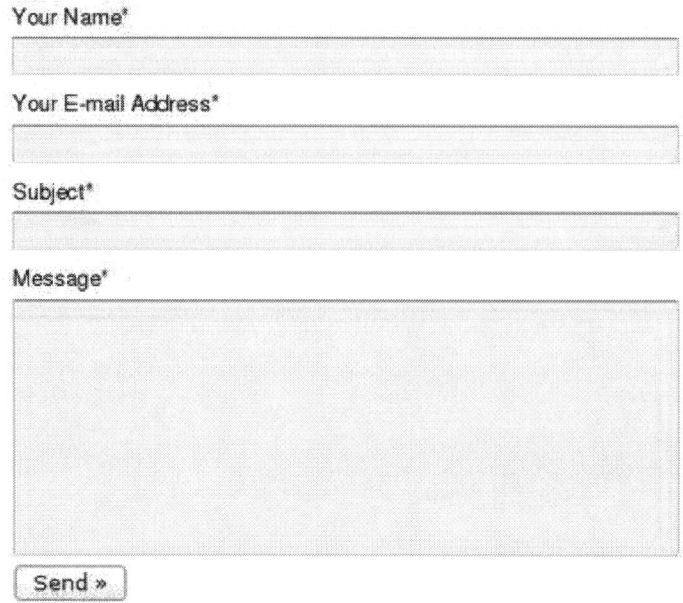

Your contact form if you use the plugin

Now Everything is Coming Along Nicely....

Heck yes! Booyah! Now that you have both your zip code and your mailing address communicating all you can do is build upon this foundation. By now you should have your pages setup, your contact form functioning to make sure that in the case that the people who visit your website decide to ask questions or make inquiries they will be able to reach you.
Now it's time to customize the look and feel of your website so that you can wow anybody who visits your website and while also making it easier for them to look around and navigate your site.

Step 9: Select your WordPress Theme

WordPress is AMAZING! You will get unlimited options available at your fingertips when it comes to customizing your website's entire look and feel. There are literally thousands of themes that will allow you to complete the look you want for your personal website or blog.

If you are looking for a theme for a regular blog and not a personal website, here are some great places to find high quality themes:

- ThemeForest
- StudioPress
- ElegantThemes
- Official WordPress theme directory
- DIYThemes

I have gone out and found 3 themes that would work well for you if you are setting up a WordPress personal resume or CV website. There are literally **endless** options available so this is just a starting point.

1. Moje

Get more information on the Moje template

2. FlexyVcard

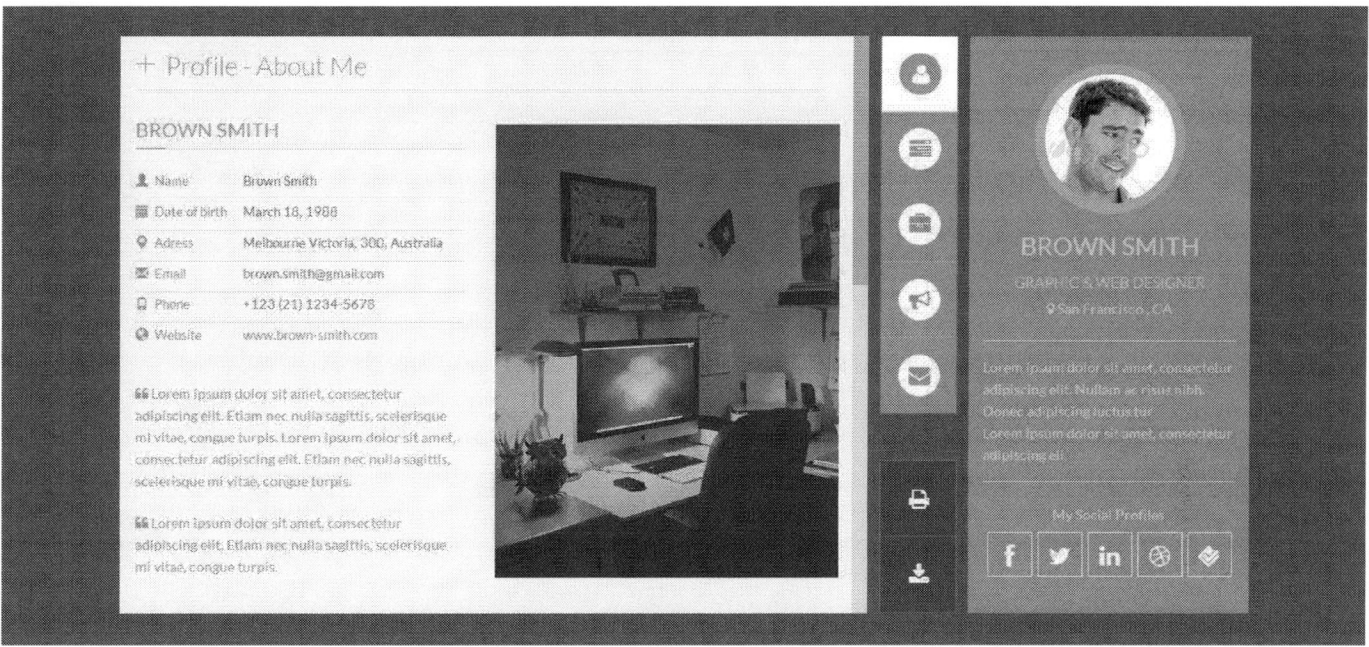

Get more information on the FlexyVcard WordPress template

3. MilzinCard - Responsive Vcard Template

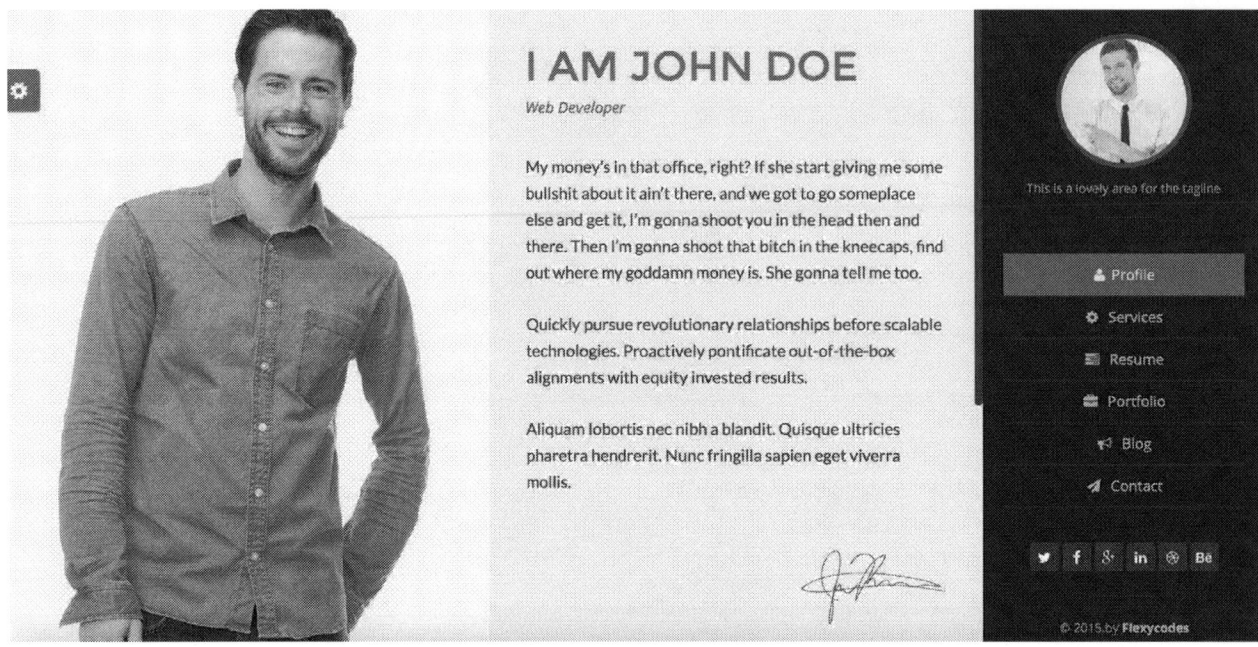

Get more information on the MilzinCard responsive Vcard template

4. CvCard

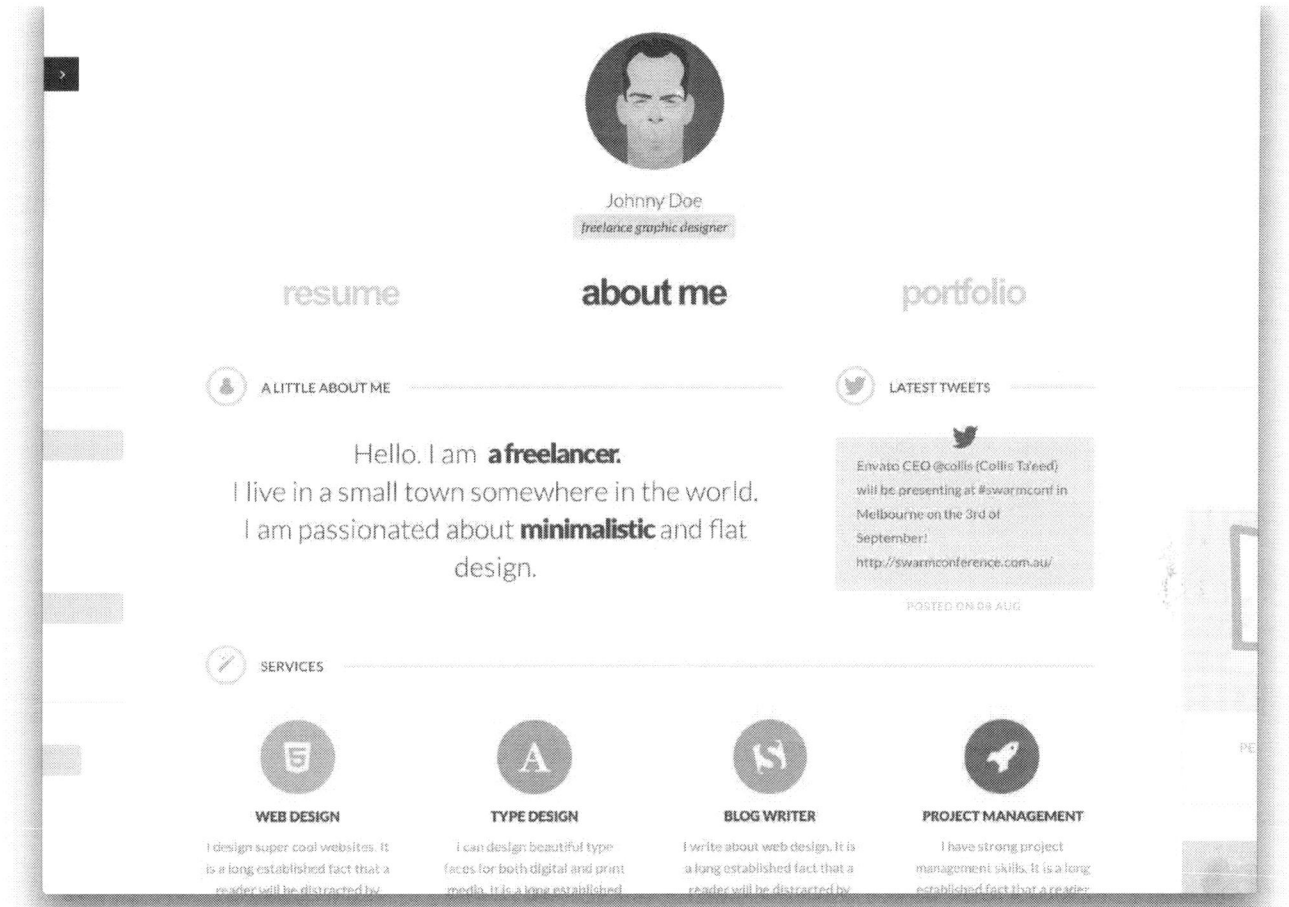

Get more information on the CvCard template

The options are **limitless**. So feel free to look around and soon enough you will find something that tickles your fancy! If you find a theme that comes with a built-in **contact page**, you will have the opportunity to set it up without having to use the contact plugin.

Step 10: Installing Your WordPress Theme (No Need to use FTP!)

After you have found your theme, you will be able to download it to your computer in .zip format. You can install your WordPress theme through the WP dashboard, sometimes uploading the theme through the WordPress dashboard does not work, so what I usually do (and would suggest you do) is to install your theme through your hosting company's cPanel. Here is how it's done:

1. Login to your JustHost cPanel
2. Under the **Files** tab, click on **File Manager**

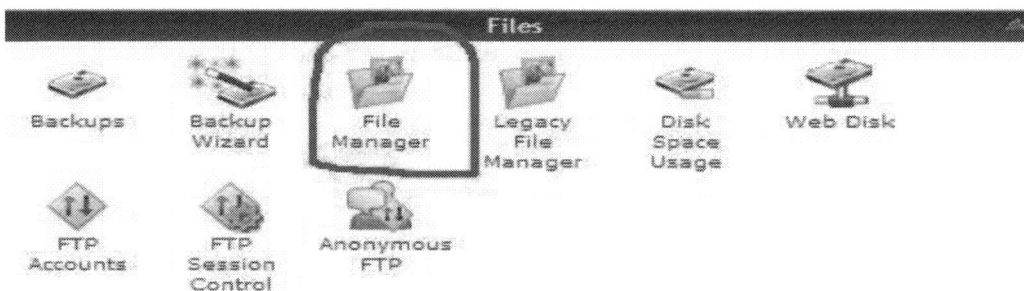

3. Click on the **Public_html** located on the left hand side of the **File Manager** to access your domain name folder

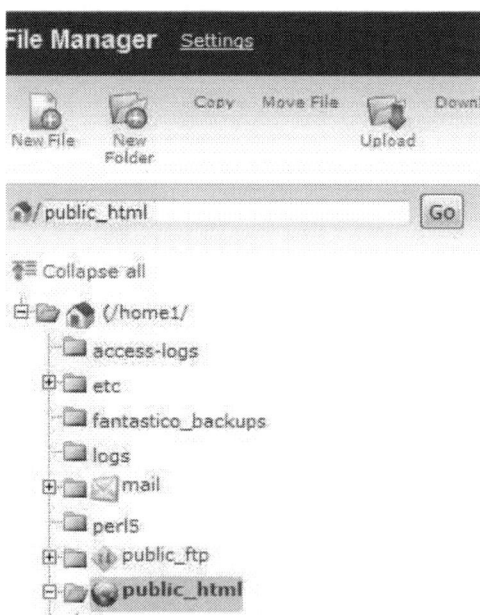

4. Once inside the domain name folder, find the folder labelled as **Wp-Content**, click on that.

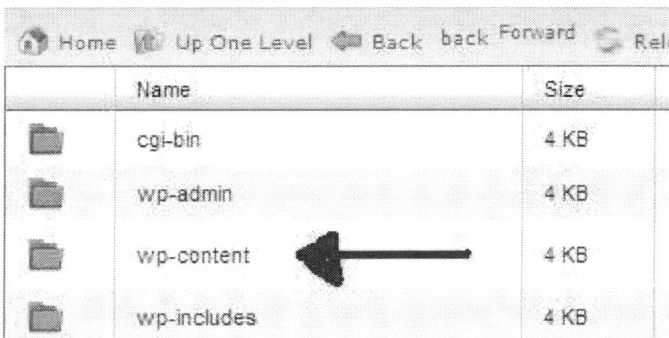

5. You will see a folder labelled **Themes**, click on this folder

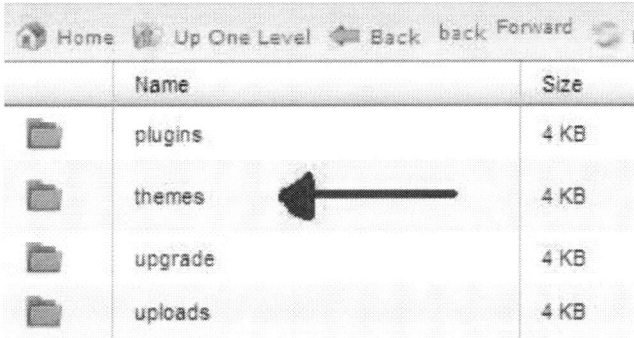

6. Now that you have the theme files in .zip format, it's time to install them. Click on the **Upload**folder located on the left hand side of the **File Manager**menu to start uploading your theme files.

30

7. Click on **Browse** to find the files in your computer storage, then click 'open'. ***Please note:*** Theme files MUST be in .zip format for the upload to work.

Permissions may default to 644, you will need to set your permissions to 755 BEFORE you browse and upload the theme files in order for the upload to work and completely upload.

8. Close the upload window and go back to the **File Manager** Themes folder. On the top right hand of the File Manager menu, you will see a folder labelled **Extract**, click on the .zip theme files you just uploaded and then click **Extract** (wait for this to comple

9. Close this window and login to your WordPress dashboard, click on the **Appearances** menu on the left hand side, then click on the Themes link and you should see your theme present in your WordPress! Click **Activate** to make your theme live. Congratulations you just successfully installed your WP theme! =)

Themes are so diverse so it's not possible for me to cover absolutely all you need to know to install a particular theme. The good news is, most high quality themes also come with readme types of files and documentations that will help you with further set up.

Step 11: Add Some Much Needed Plugins and Widgets

WordPress functions just fine by itself, however its abilities to function THAT much better depends on the types of plugins you can add to your website. I do not recommend adding just any plugin (as having too many plugins installed and active can greatly slow down your blog/website), however, there are a few essential plugins you will need for WordPress to perform at its optimum level.

To install plugins, all you have to do is go to your WordPress Dashboard and click on **Plugins** -> then **Add New** and search for the plugin you want by name -> after you have found the plugin,-> click **Install Now**-> then **Activate** the plugin after install and that all!

The following are 12 of the most recommended essential plugins you should install on your website:

1. WordPress SEO by Yoast: This plugin will really help you out with on-page SEO and getting traffic to your posts because the better positioned your keyword is , the more likely you are to get targeted traffic to your post!
2. Editorial Calendar: If you lack organization in your posting schedule, the editorial plugin is just what you need! It allows you to schedule blog posts, topics and even brainstorm what you want to write about. If you want to get things done and succeed online with WordPress, you need this for sure.
3. Privacy Policy: Looking to make more with Adsense? Did you know that adding a privacy policy page to your blog can increase your Adsense earnings. (WP has removed all the Privacy Policy plugins for whatever reason so you'll just have to create your own)
4. Google XML Sitemap: Search engines such as Ask.com, Bing, Google and Yahoo will be better able to find your blog and index it if you have an existing sitemap.
5. Broken Link Checker: This plugin will enable you to scan and find useless non-working links in your blog. It saves you the time of having to check each and every individual post for dead links. This one's a must have time saver.
6. W3 Total Cache: Improves your blog's loading speed and performance by clearing any cache that might slow things down.

7. Disqus Commenting System: If you're fed up with spammy comments, installing Disqus can cut down greatly on those pesky and annoying useless comments.
8. BackUpWordPress: It's important to backup your blog regularly (I learned this the hard way), the backup plugin makes it a breeze, it's even possible to store a few backup copies of your site. If anything happens you will be able to restore your website via the **Import** option in the **Tools** section of your WP Dashboard.
9. Wp-PageNavi: Keep your posts organized numerically by number instead of using the default 'next' or 'previous page' navigation style. This makes your blog more user friendly.
10. Better WP Security: Keep yourself protected from hackers (I had my very first blog destroyed by hackers and boy did I learn a very tough lesson). Every WP site I own used this particular plugin.
11. Limit Login Attempts -A really important plugin that helps to protect your WordPress blog/website from pesky hackers who use sophisticated scripts that try to hack your blog by guessing the password over and over again.
12. Social Media Widget –This plugin will enable you to add links to all of your social media profiles and show the icons of any added social media site on the sidebar of your website.

Before I forget!

Remember to add Google Analytics to your website as you will want to track the visitors that come to your site and the stats you will get from the Google Analytics plugin will enable you to see how many visits/day to your site, where the visits come from, how long on average are visitors staying on your site etc. Wpmu.org also has a tutorial about how you can setup Google Analytics here.

Before you install your WordPress plugins, search for them through the WordPress Plugin Directory if a plugin has a star rating of 3 or less, it might have issues such as the owner is not updating it properly, it could be broken – or worst case scenario, it might expose your blog to cyber attacks due to security vulnerabilities it can open up once you install it. So be careful out there in the inter-webs.

Let's Add Some Widgets!

Ahem!-What are widgets first of all? Widgets are the elements that show up on any website that is 'widget enabled' , usually widgets are displayed on the sidebar but with some WordPress themes you can also display widgets on the footer area. You can add sponsorship banners, ad network banners etc. to your widget area if you run a blog and **if you are creating a personal website**, you can add your social media profiles on the widget area. You already have a few widgets on display if you look at your site, these include: **Recent Posts**, **Category** and **Meta**.

To edit or modify any of the widgets on your website, simply follow these steps:

1. On your WordPress Dashboard, click on the **Appearance**option, then click on **Widgets**.

2. You will see a **widget area**normally located on the right hand side of the screen on your theme.

3. Drag the widgets you would like to display from the middle area and onto the correct boxes. (If you want to paste HTML code, use the widget labelled as **Text**)

4. Refresh your main website to see the changes.

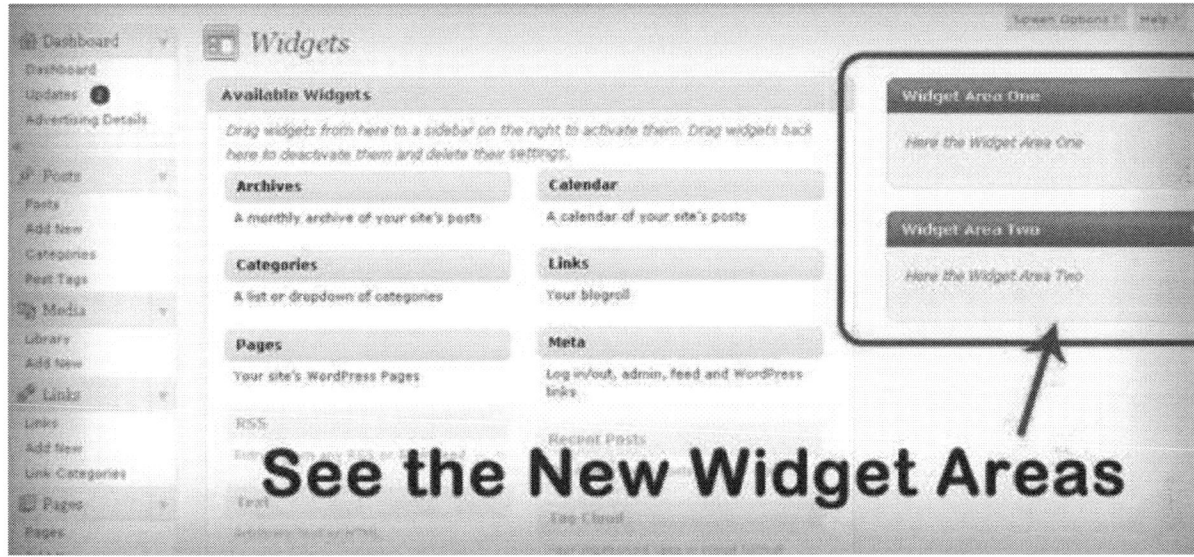

If you are creating a personal website, the following are a few essential and complementary widgets you might want to have on display:

- **Social Media Widget** -With this widget, you get to put social media icons that link to your online social media profiles by using the social media plugin doing so is a breeze.
- **Links** -Build a network of like-minded people or friends and link to their websites, this is also a great way to network within your industry.

- **Text** –If you have anything that contains code/HTML, you can put it in the text widget. You can also add a short bio or add your tweets if you are using the Twitter Profile widget. You can do whatever you please with this!

Congratulations you have now created your own website!

By now you have a fully functioning website! I feel I should congratulate you as this is something to be proud of. You followed the instructions from beginning to end and now you have created all your pages, set your contact page, installed a knockout theme, added and activated a few great plugins – not to mention a few complementary widgets on your sidebar.

Congratulations are also in order because your Internet street cred is off the chains as you have managed to transform yourself into a more interesting person and a preferably more attractive applicant and candidate to any job you may desire to apply or interview

If you are building a personal site instead of a blog, you can also do the following in order to get the maximum benefits from your personal site:

-> Put your URL somewhere on any of paper resumes or any resumes you send out
-> Input your URL into your Twitter bio
-> Create some mind-blowing and memorable business cards (don't forget to include your URL)
-> Add your personal website's URL to your online social network profiles such as LinkedIn, Google+, Facebook, Pinterest etc.
-> Get active on social networks and join or start like-minded blogs, groups, forums get in the know and stay open for opportunities by keeping an open mind!

Made in the USA
Middletown, DE
21 July 2020

13333497R00024